# Glimmers of Light

Decima Wraxall

# Glimmers of Light

*Glimmers of Light*
ISBN 978 1 76109 270 1


First published 2022 by
GINNINDERRA PRESS
PO Box 3461 Port Adelaide 5015
www.ginninderrapress.com.au

# Contents

## Tapestry

Snow-capped peaks in Europe burn into my
memory. Glimpsed once, and treasured forever.
Time unfolds beneath the wings of my 747,
a hum gives way to the thump of arrival.

Found treasures evoke marvel and delight.
A small smooth stone from Beauvais calls forth an
unfinished cathedral. Chestnuts gathered from La
Place de la Concorde bring their roasted flavour.

A silver friendship ring, rescued from dust, whispers
of Paris, a camping, and chestnut trees. Red stones
retrieved from sand at Cap du Dramont, on the Riviera,
bring back ancient villas, and the splash of briny sea.
The White Cliffs at Dover yield chalk, the aroma

of distant classrooms, and the sting of a ruler.
The red and gold dance of trees at Kensington
Gardens reminds me it's almost time for home.
In the shiver of autumn, leaves float free,
drifting to earth, one by one. At ochre bluffs, wide

horizons, and deserts of my native land, I ponder
the tapestry of travel.
Laughter juggles with wonder. The spiritual walls of Iona
dissolve into the heartbreak of broken dreams
at Port Arthur. Mourned, in and out of dank cells.

## Culture Clash

i

Great-grandparents fled the humiliations of humble birth. Denied the
privilege of green acres, and fine houses, the might of lords, they
bade farewell to kith and kin. Their hopes lay in a land of eucalypts

and wattle. Granted small plots of land by the British crown.
Sweat, axe, mattock and saw built huts, fences and more. They
strode free, masters of an alien colony. But their hungry eyes lusted
for vast, empty space. Oblivious to the needs of another race.

ii

The whities claimed hallowed places. A sacred ceremony ground, with
river views, the perfect spot for a slab-hut pub and village. Oblivious
to the pride of indigenous tribes, and aeons of harmony, with land,

tree and emu. Carved trees whispered of didge music and dancing
in the dust. Dreamtime ghosts and shadows murmured, of dignity
and history, black ownership unremarked. Spears and shields hissed

outrage. Muskets cracked, seeping the red of fallen totems. Under their
tender care, diverse fauna had survived and thrived. Farmers seized the
rich flood plains of indigenous tribes. Harvests of native grains and yams

succumbed to plough, foreign crops and cattle. Native fish traps fell
into disuse, a novelty. Cobwebbed now, hollow trees spoke of smoked
perch and eels, cured for later. Native plants were seen as weeds.

Vitamin-rich fruit rotted on the ground. Prized seeds, once made safe by burbling water, ignored. Trading-routes crisscrossed this great land. Paths eroded by feet and time.

Barbed wire. Certificates of ownership. Hunting grounds
out of bounds. Invaders ate kangaroo, fish too.
And, helpless, tribes died of starvation…

## Another Day in the Serengeti

Under the blistering gaze of the African sun, we see
lions circle.
Wildebeest rasping cries. A barrage of battering heads
and thrusting horns.
Hooves thunder, dust swirls, flanks heave.
The big cats regroup,
this storm of rippling muscles and stiletto teeth.
The herd angle,
paw the earth, shielding their young.
It's a melee of hungry cats

and snorting beasts, But lions stalk,
edging a half-grown
calf from the mob. It freezes, eyes agape.
A surge of weight and ripping claws drag it down.
The wail
of struggling hair and bone. Shocked glances, tourists
shiver.

A lioness rips open the chest. The calf's heart flies into the
air, spurting red.
She catches the prize in slavering jaws, gulps it whole.
Cubs, covered
in gore, join in the fun, a first taste of flesh. The feast
done, lions recline,
sated, among the prickle of thorn trees. Later, we dine
at our five-star
hotel. And masticate steaks, blood leaking onto
pristine plates.

# Jaunty

Jaunty angled hats, faces aglow, they march away,
to country's call.
Mired in mud at the Western Front, the Last Post plays –
it never stops. Raw boots and hopes, join the fray.
Keen as blades, yet to shave. Shells scream,

and troops shiver, cursing the endless, ring of bells.
Cannons roar at Ypres and El Alamein.
Bullets or shrapnel, it's all the same. Hot
their rifles, red the flood. And red the poppies,
flourishing, in their blood.

Silent sentinels, stand here and there. Leafless,
broken limbs, beware. Birdsong flew from this poem,
guessing where it was going. Another soldier
plunges and falls, calling for his mother.
A litany of the lost, rises, in the ache of skies.

Ships head for home. Silent in the shudder,
of what they've seen. Suffering etched
in old-young eyes. Recalling too much,
forgetting too little.
Waves roll, motors hum. Bunks shout

and sweat, awake half the night. Men
laugh too loud, smoke too much.
And dare not cry. Though there's a tear
in every eye. Shouts, cheers, hugs at the wharf.
A shadow, invisible, to me and you, the 1918 Spanish flu…

## Undeclared War

Beds and lockers, scrape and groan. Moved now, ready. Antiseptic tang.
Make calculations. Staff search for ventilators, IV stands, PPEs…
Elective surgery cancelled, ready for a hurricane of folk in extremis.
Utilise every medical weapon, send those smallsters away.
Hazmat suit warriors, wait, accept their fate. Masked, plastic shields
and gloves in place. Ambulances wail into chaos. Day and night,
it's a fight to save the afflicted. The ward noticeboard glows red.
Forget surgeons, ENT, haematologists – just doctors and nurses.

Long, searing shifts. Fifteen to twenty emergencies arrive each day.
Covid-inflicted pneumonia sweats and groans, gasping for air.
Ventilators rare as gold, rationed for those most likely to make it.
A flatline beeeeeeeep…

Safety protocols, vital PPEs ,missing in action. Makeshift, garbage-bag
scrubs. And hang onto your mask – if you have one. Forget discarding it
after use. Another doctor, a second nurse, test Covid-positive. Beep, beep…
Beeeeeep… Another bed to carbolise. Another linen change.
Legs and bodies one big ache – and that's the staff. No time to
grieve. And wipe those tears from burning eyes.

# Aflame

My horoscope said, interesting love life
Until forty
At eighteen, it seemed a good deal

I never guessed that love flames in the human
Heart, beyond the shiver of youth and vitality,
Magic seized in the wake of lost chances.

Defying oxygen-deprived heights, and snow-capped
peaks, we drifted into the wonder of eternity. My
fantasy reclaimed, I quaked in the ache

of your smile. The tremor of your touch. Giddy, foolish,
carefree me. We drank nectar from our golden cup.
Clasped in starched white, gifted with your tender

embrace. Those eyes and the hands you loved me by.
Moans, sighs, laughter. Mutual exhilaration. We
Savoured the heights of ecstasy. Jewel of autumn delight.
Plucked, from the undertow of age and time.

## Sacrifice

A world of abandoned hugs, the intimacy
of a kiss. Handshakes out, shoulder bumps
the go. Touch, the gift that makes
us human, denied. Lost to social

distancing and isolation.
We crave the freedom to gather,
mix and mingle, sing, dance and laugh –

all our birthrights, until snatched away.
Stolen by an invisible foe we cannot
smell or touch. Folks say loss aversion

makes some reluctant to wear a mask.
It's not much to ask, and the life you
save, may be your own. Doctors

and nurses have worn them for years,
without problem or risk. What, I
wonder, do mask deniers fear?

Let's smile, and do the things we should.
Take time to learn the art of sacrifice –
knowing it's for the greater good.

## Dense With Smoke

Rifle fire. Breaking glass. The hotel screams.
Heart thumping against my ribs and chest,
I note the shooting direction.

Cops taught me that, last siege.
Or was it the one before?
I'm up to number four.

My best friend, ashen-faced, rushes towards
the doors. No, wait, Danny, wait!
But he flees. A fusillade of bullets.

I bolt for the side door. Rip off my red T-shirt.
Bright colours attract attention. Scale a wall.
Unobserved. Blood drips from my hand.
Superficial scratch, not worth a mention.

Barefoot, I zigzag, running along the beach.
It's dense with smoke. Zing of gunfire,
I gasp for breath in acrid air.

A rat on the run, I slither into a drain.
Stutter of gunfire. Sirens. Yells.
It's cramped, damp and mouldy.
One hour? Two? Who knew…

No shouts. No shots. No boots running past.
The joyous slosh of waves. Shriek of a gull.
Trembling, I slide to the entrance.
Fumble for my phone. Dial my best buddy.
Danny doesn't pick up.

## Mismanaged

US Doctors livid. Pandemic preparation time
squandered. A major part of the catastrophe avoidable,
patients put at unnecessary risk.
Trump's rhetoric hampered Infection control.
All's well. Back to normal by Easter.

Months of inaction. Failure to create
and administer diagnostic tests. Upper Respiratory
Infections gasped into hospitals. Covid-19 pneumonia.

Massive viral loads. Nurses, doctors, paramedics
at risk. This pandemic handled the pandemic.
Trump fiddled with his golf balls, sleepwalking,
tone deaf, while Corona multiplied and took flight.

## Sons at Easter

A frown of clouds howl outside. We chatter
around the Easter table, aglow in the flow of wishes.
A family, in all but blood. Italian. Greek. Irish…
The aroma of incense and Easter Buns, shadowed by loss.
Mourning He who died on the cross. Red Easter eggs. Chocolate-coated
friends. Colleagues all, we nurse the old , the crippled
and the sick. Share rare moments of reflection. Break the bread,
drink the wine. Tina frowns. My son, in Yugoslavia. Eighteen.
Out of work. No profession. She stops. Stretton Uskrus…

Buona Pasqua says Marie from Italy. She from the Emerald
Isles dreams green potato fields. Bluebells. And the Irish harp.
Anna short hair. We saw her kiss the dog goodbye –
but not her husband. A whisper, *Les Meilleurs Vouex.*
Sighs for Lebanon. Smoke plumes. Houses aflame. Rising death toll.
Laughs for her son in Sydney. Studies dentistry. His hands fumble.
Watch your tongue and your teeth.
Happy Easter, say the Aussie crew.
The Greek ladies share a glance. Troubled faces. Calo Pasqua in low voice.
Whispering of a hill cemetery. Distant isle. Glitter of the Aegean Sea.

Voula's hair marble-grey. It paled from black
overnight.
Her son, nineteen. Buried in white
marriage costume, though he wasn't wed.
Gold gleam. Third finger, left hand.
Her piercing howls of lament resonate
from the Greek church to our memory.
Shivering into tears. Edging, down
glacial window glass.

## Critical Care

Specialist shocked at how patients get sick so darned quick.
Morning a mild cough. Short of breath. A headache.
Within hours, sever lung inflammation, gasping
for air. Stiff respiratory tissue is the issue. Difficult

to get enough oxygen to the blood. On life support,
ventilators disperse high concentrations of oxygen-
enriched air, the difference between life and death.
But the longer on life support, the less chance to survive.

Control measures ignored.
Hundreds of thousands will die. We must educate
the public to take Corona seriously, before it's too late.
Social distancing and isolation the only way to slow

infections. Ventilators crucial. Consensus asks for
more face masks. But the US government
forces blue states to fight red over supplies.
Tent hospitals erected in Central Park.

Staff PPEs garbage bags and home-made
masks. Businesses retool, producing sanitisers,
masks and gowns Two hundred sailors infected,
on the *Roosevelt* aircraft carrier. Nowhere on board

for crew to isolate. In a climate of magical thinking, the captain's
urgent plea for help ignored. Letter released. Hierarchy fury. Captain
relieved of his duty… But the crew cheered their hero off the ship.
Applauding self-sacrifice and humanity, in an age of ignorance and greed.

## The Burrell Collection

It's easy to see why it took a lifetime collecting these riches.
We admire silver porcelain and ceramics of the Ming and other
dynasties. Imagine the stitches of tapestries and brushstrokes
of paintings, masters of every hand. The architect garnered
Elizabethan doorways and French windows, enriching the fabric

of the building. Ablaze with light from walls of glass,
fields of bluebells and chestnut trees dance indoors,
part of the display space. Skylights juggle rays, between
layered timber beams. Antique stained glass is aglow with red
orange and blue yellow too, with colours of every hue. The
technology which gave birth to these early and brilliant

examples of their art perished, with craftsmen, dead
from the plague. Impressionist paintings chat with carved
oak chairs and sideboards, heavy with history. We applaud a
solid oak dining table. Gaze in delight at a carved oak ceiling,
with acorns and leaves, to rival those of the living tree

I caressed the linen-fold panelling. and could see why
Burrell moved from a cottage to a castle, just for his
treasure's sake. And now it's all out there, for the pleasure
of Glasgow, and those of every nation– the Burrell Collection

## Logical But Flawed

Water drips from the hairs on my arms. Hands
held high to avoid contamination. I can't wait
to begin. I guess this adrenalin rush is what an actor feels
before he strides on stage. The nurse helps me don
my gown. I pull on my gloves. Surgeon, king

of my domain. Minions adjust the mirrored overhead light.
Grasping the scalpel, fractured images explain the process
to my juniors. Jokey. Calm.
Floating on the easy insouciance of experience.
Beep beep, beep. My patient's
elective surgery isn't serious. It's barely over, and I make to
take off my gloves. 'Beep…beep…beep…beeep!
BEEEEEEEEEEEEEEEEEEEEEEEEP!' Flat line on the screen.

Code blue. Failed attempts to revive him.
His life flashes through my mind. Guilt. Agonised
thoughts of the patient's family. How can I
explain this loss?

The theatre doors burst open. His wife, wild-eyed. My
husband came to me in the waiting-room. Out of his body. He's
not dead, Doctor… I'm about to hustle her out, when the jagged
heart line leaps back. Beep, beep, beep. Colour rushes
into his cheeks. Staff exchange glances. What are
the chances…

The patient tells of theatre interactions, the resuscitation.
Hairs prickle on my head. I thought, But you were brain dead…
The intern storms out. I'll not listen to many more of this.
But I step closer. Tell me more…

Is medicine following a logical, but flawed model
of our Universe?
Could consciousness begin in the brain?
Or our brain seek consciousness to survive?

# Tsunami

Empty corridors. Tick tock tick. Gloved hands clasped. Waiting.
        Protective glasses. Shields. Hazmat suits.
Ambulance wail. Covid-19 explodes into the ward.
Ten times more contagious
        than a bad flu. Drenching sweats. Sore throat.
Aches and pains.
Patients gulping oxygen in intensive care.
        Wartime triage. Who lives? Who dies?
Access comorbidities. Age of patient.
        No miracles.

Operations cancelled.
        Display board names all code red.
Days merge with nights. Swab results arrive   Positive   Positive
        Positive.
The emergency room teeters on the edge of collapse.
        Fifteen, twenty seriously ill patients admitted every day.

Always the same diagnosis. Bilateral interstitial pneumonia.
        Not just the old. Younger patients intubated in
intensive care.
The ECMO heart and lung machine treats the critically ill
        Extracts blood. Re-oxygenates. Returns it to body.
Hoping the virus will abate. Let the lungs heal

No more surgeons, bone specialists, urologists.

Only a single team of doctors and nurses. Groping, through a tsunami of crises.

More than a thousand positives in Lombardy.

Don't panic. Don't underestimate. And staff shake their heads at Facebook complaints.

Home isolation, lack of the gym, and they can't swim…

Humanitas Gavazzeni hospital, Bergamo, Italy

## My Invisible Friends

Daddy said, No more war.
Invasion fears are over, thank the Lord.
I couldn't wait to tell the others,

my invisible friends. Jim shed tears
of joy. I told you we would win. He hugged
my rag doll, Jemima. She lay there for all to see.
About time, said she. Baby, it seemed, was too young

to ken. Lamp Spider, scowled and shouted, Bring back
the bombs! I want the bombs. Cousin Poppy called him,
A nasty piece of work. Oliver, my special friend,
switched genders, according to whim – a girl, that day.

Don't sit there, Mum, I cried. You'll
squash Oliver. My mother frowned, but switched chairs. Later,
she called me to lunch. I'm playing with Oliver. She stamped

her foot. Stop talking about that silly Oliver. Come to the
table at once. Next time I raised the manifestation,
of my phantom friends, Mum gave a slow

shake of her head. Killed in a car crash, I fear.
My eyes widened. But…Oliver says…
She's dead, I'm afraid.

Not she, Mum. He.
I don't care if it's he or she. Oliver is dead – they all are.
Jim, Baby, Jemima, and that dreadful Lamp Spider.
I don't want to hear of them again.

At five, perhaps I held Jemima and cried.
Surely, they were alive…
In secret, I tried to contact them all again,
But the magic had died.

## Ventilate

2020 took hospitals back, back to a world where masks,
hygiene, sanitation, social distancing and isolation were
medical gold. Weapons, against the woes of plague,
well before virus and bacteria had a name. Florence

Nightingale knew a thing or two about what hospitals
must do, to keep death at bay. But in her day, miasma
took the blame for fatal illness, not microbes. Large

windows, opened top and bottom, to blow away foul air.
High ceilings in huge wards helped ventilation.
Big droplets from coughs and sneezes fell to the floor,

mopped away. And aerosols, afloat for hours, were
carried outside, on friendly breezes. Modern hospital
four-bed wards boast
low ceilings, at their peril, with small closed windows.

Hot days rush of chill, recycled air, makes the
best petri dish the Covid-19 virus could wish,
snatching the frail and ill. And tiny tea rooms for staff,
smile a Corona welcome, ready for an easy kill.

# A Walk in the Sun

Daddy stumbled into the kitchen. The stink of booze,
emanating from his pores. I felt sick to the stomach.
He'd collected bread, the mailbag… And cradled
two bottles of wine.
Mum's eyes bulged. Aren't you ever going to stop?

He slurred, Just a little please…to tide me over.
The cork squeaked, with finality – I can hear it still.
Dad downed the tiny glass in a gulp. A walk in the
sun will do me good. He shambled off, shoulders
hunched, clutching a corn-bag rug.
An image flashed: my father, proud and tall.
It almost broke my heart.

Mum shook with rage. What's he up to now?
A cloud of dust swirled across the creek. Jack-the-mail, stopped
his Land Rover by a culvert. Purveyor of illicit grog…
Mum's anger shrank with the dying light. Your father should
be back – in his state he'd never survive. In a tangle of tussocks,
Victor found six bottles of red wine. Two empty.

We spread out. I squelched through
the swamp. Frogs croaked of reeds and rusty
water. DAAD! DADDDY!
Tea tree clawed at bare arms and legs. Plovers scream. Whoosh!
I leapt in fright. Twilight edged with ice.
And I feared the chill of night
N…not a body? My heart thumped against its cage of bone.
A shadowed log, not the human form… I breathed again.

Victor's loud Cooee. Mum at my side, we gained the top paddock.
She whispered, How did…did he stagger so far? My father deathly pale.
Slumped on his damp rug. My teeth chittered. Dad isn't… Couldn't be…
Mum gave voice to my fears. He's not… Not dead…?
My brother sniggered. Dead drunk.
And kicked away an empty bottle of Johnny Walker.

## Delirium Tremens

We half-carried, half-dragged Dad back home.
Helped him to bed.
His yells and shouts struck the sleeping night.
I felt for my mother.

Our dawn house lurched, seeking Dad's lost soul.
He tottered to the gate, rushed back, wild-eyed.
Don't let her get me.
Mum's frown. Stop that nonsense! She tempted him with porridge.
His every muscle had the shakes. The spoon clattered
to the floor. I can't, Genn.
You must eat something… But he couldn't.
We plied him with fluids.

Mum rode off with Victor to muster cattle.
I took over, squaring my shoulders.
Terrified my father might not make it.
Would chicken broth and time give him another reprieve?
Go to bed, Dad.

But terror had him by the darting eyes. Come with me,
please. Please…
I led my father, child-man, into his bedroom.
Tucked the sheets around the tremor of his six
foot-six frame. He pleaded. Make sure the window's closed.
I don't want her to get me…

Dad, there's nobody…
I…I've seen her… A mermaid, down by the lake of wine.
Dressed in clothes of many hues – trying to outdo your mother.
Unsure whether to laugh or weep.
Sleep, Dad, sleep. I'm right here. You'll be safe.

## Corona NY

Corona sharpens its thorns.
A breath lost, in the ancient winds.
The Spanish flu, Aids…
And now, Corona. Invisible. Smaller than a grain
of sand. They hunt in packs. Invade. Mutate.
Their killing fields know no borders.
From a stranger's topple in the street –
to Holy Orders.

Wail. Rescue is on the run. The old, middle-aged,
the young – Corona infections reach a peak.
And tent wards moan in Central Park.
Respirators scarce, running hot.
Masks, gowns and PPEs too few. Victims falling
by the score. Lost too soon to this Corona war.
A colleague died, just last night. Our medical team
enhance their fight.

The deadly dancer skips on, from hand, to mouth, to lung.
Beep. Words shadowed, in the gasp for air. Beep.
Staff stagger, blinking, from the glare. Beep. Fluorescent lights.
Flat line on a screen. Drip. Tubes stretch to patients' arms. Drip.
IV stands in the hall. Nurses adjust the flow. Not too fast,

nor too slow. Drip. Government failures
fuelled the toll, leaving Corona virus on a roll.
But, wait. Measures to isolate began early, not late.
And mortality rates are on the wane.
Nurses sag. Yawn. And smile.

## Dystopia

Lightning struck the tree of society
split asunder the trunk of liberty and decency,
fuelled a nation's debt-ridden journey.

Half of the nation's population survive
from one food handout to another, while an
inefficient social system drifts into economic

depression. A weakened tree leans into poverty,
nurtures despair, seeking help that isn't there.
A society of servants can't support res publica:

driving other folk's cars, cleaning strangers' homes,
bringing the latest luxury to a tyranny of the super-rich.
Lost hopes destroy innovation, institutions shatter

and fail. Don't wait for intelligent debate. The U-curve
loiters in the wings of a dying economy, wearing
jackboots, no bell curve to stop neo-authoritarian
dystopia, in this assault on democracy.

# Easter in a Time of Covid

Forget get-togethers and get aways.
Forget your long weekend up the coast.
Let road deaths take a break. Covid tolls

the knell, from another hill. The United
States rate overtakes Italy. Dozens buried
in trenches, without friends or family.

Sixty doctors and nurses self-isolate. Fourteen
days… Fifty people cop a thousand
dollar fine for breaking isolation.

Folk exercise to build their immune system.
More deaths from the *Ruby Princess*.
Police enquiry underway. How were

hundreds of passengers allowed to disembark
without quarantine? Let fly interstate
and overseas – not even basic checks.

Good Friday churches closed. Online
prayers. The Pope speaks alone
from the Vatican Basilica.

Elated, repatriated Australians arrive from Peru,
and Cambodia. Aussies in India feel abandoned.
Desperate to get home. Price hikes on fares.

Flights cancelled. Weary smiles. Some high risk –
if gran got sick, most likely she'd die. Private
charters cost too much. Bumped off flights.

Hopes cancelled. And families play board
games. Erect tents on lawns. To stay safe,
they holiday and pray at home.

# I Love

I love the smell of petrichor after a fall of rain.
The susurrus of a wander through the bush,
in our back paddock .The smell of eucalypt on
the hot summer air.

My skin sings at the apricity in winter,
when the sun peeps through a scowl of clouds.
I love the wide country skies, pink from horizon
to horizon, at sunset, or in the east, at dawn.

I love the golden veil of evening on the distant
hill, and its treed reflections in the lake.
The laugh of a kookaburra, praising the joy,
of being alive

I love to watch the ripple of muscles,
when horses frolic and play.
Beguiled by the velvet touch
of the bay's nose, sniffing my hand.

I love willy wagtails dancing sweet-pretty-creature,
in the fragrance of red roses, lavender and lilac.
And a strut of fairy wrens, boast blue waistcoats,
to the jubilation of a robin redbreast's song.

# Once a Spook

We've enough Novichok to destroy half the population.
I use only the best. About to silence an annoying pest.
Spare him your sympathy or tears. He's defamed me
for years. Minions know
to follow my orders. Forget democracy and borders.

He'll ebb away with a gut-wrenching
spew. Muscle spasms, out of breath,
pinpoint pupils. Affects the brain, too. I'll spare
you the details. At my nod, he'll groan and pray to
his God. If he has one.

Husband and Father, that's me. I buy ice creams
for my kids.
Take my wife to the doctor.
But I've one rule: never let my heart
rule the head. Now, I hug my little girl
and tuck her into bed.

## Merciless

No guns or missiles inform this slaughter.
A war without rank or order. Invisible. Deadly.
Masks, gloves and gowns are few. A ventilator fail
on the wards. While patients test positive in hordes.
Forget your riches and your power –
victim's deaths rising by the hour. The deadly RNA takes trips
in ships and on airplanes, too.
Travellers isolate, fourteen days to know their fate.

When a Ruby and a Princess left so many infected, it wasn't expected.
And there's the tale of nuptial bliss. A bridal kiss shared with sister,
brother, friend and mother. Brought a virus zing
to champagne toasts. Hurting the ones she loved the most.
Home a prison and a shelter. Avoid the virus, helter-skelter.
Help slow the march on the street. Mortality
crowns restless feet.

Covid-19 clutches tighter than a lover. Sees them suffocate and suffer.
A black bag tower lurks outside the door.
Before the day is over, there'll be more.
Seldom has the River Styx endured such a fix. Farewell Elmo,
Fred and Auntie Lizzie. The ferryman feels quite dizzy –
no time now to take his cuppa.
Another load is on the water. Husband, son and
baby daughter.

## Royal Tour

Miranda travelled in style, like an African Queen,
on human elephants. Her mum and dad took  turns
to act as pachyderm. Too heavy for granny, she rode

in their backpack, protected by a navy spotted
sun brolly. The toddler's mode of transport
brought smiles, envious glances, and phone pictures,

from weary hikers at Kakadu, through Katherine
and to Alice Springs. In restaurants she held court,
making eyes at other diners. Waitresses carried

her around, beguiled by her cheeky smile
and giggles. While we took a bite
of crocodile with bush spices.

## Near Death Experience

A landscape of purple flowers the most
vibrant colours I'd ever seen.
My journey of validation and awakening,

among undulating images of profound love.
A soul floating free of pain and misery,
my ravaged body on the bed.
Shadow beings shared their phenomenal
knowledge of the universe.

All my questions answered.
No need for words. In this state of heightened
consciousness, I learnt to interpret
and share the depth of feelings. A warm
yet detached spiritual entity,
able to honour others, and myself. A state
of being, not judging. Living moment to moment.

Nothing on this earth compares to my
glimpse of the divine. Drifting,
in the flow of eternal energy,
and unconditional love.

## Pachyderm

Queen Miranda sat on tussocks beside the red dirt path,
at sacred Uluru. Her daddy needed a break and my daughter
sighed over the ache in her back and shoulders – I laughed.

Life of a pachyderm is not an easy one. She left to fetch
the stroller. Chubby hands grabbed oesophagus-sized
pebbles. No! Daddy crackled dry leaves in the swish

of an errant breeze. Caressed by her giggles, I sought to tease.
Just for fun, and to distract our little one, decorating Daddy's
straw hat with twigs and gum nuts. He feigned tears.

How did she guess gran was being naughty? Small fingers
removed them, one by one, and Mummy trundled
back in the afternoon sun, to laughter and cheers.

## Special Edition

National holiday. Conga lines, dancing in Piccadilly
Circus and Pall Mall. Street parties, bunting,
royals wave from balcony – seven times.

Shouts, cheers, hugs, waltzing in towns
all over Britain. Couples kiss at the top
of lamp posts. Churchill's victory speech,

unconditional surrender. Rule Britannia,
Britannia rules the waves. Spotlight on
St Paul's. Cathedrals, symbol

of resistance. Our boys free to return
home. Thank God it's over. A shiver
for our sons who didn't make it.

We'll meet again one fine day. Her eyes blur,
lump in throat, squeeze hands, silent prayer. A
whisper,
It's more like a funeral than sacred jubilation.

Nazi Party emblem shot away. Church bells
chime, the first time since 1940. VE Day, one
of the greatest celebrations in history.

## Long Nights and Daily Pressers

It's seen in the faces of the stricken. Farewell
video shared, with family.
Forget black crêpe and the aroma of lilies.
Makeshift parlour, refrigerated truck.
Mother interred, taken before her time. No holy rites.
No loved ones to mourn, or share tales of her life.

Twenty-something survivor. Before this plague
he ran for miles. Now tired and breathless
climbing stairs. Job lost, plans on hold.
His invisible foe won't reward the bold.
Blokes curse lockdowns and closed pubs.

Shouts for freedom adrift, on the breeze. Fists,
kicks and flags defy orders. Girls sneak
across closed borders. Handcuffs press charges.
Bravado caught by the throat.

Stress etches politicians' faces. Weary in the wake
of long nights, and daily pressers, they weigh their options.
Positives down, but death rates up. Isolation
is a waiting game
Stand firm against fools and doubters.

Implore cooperation. Take the red footsteps,
of social distancing. Wear your mask,
stop further advances of a deadly foe.

## Glitter

Scarred hills, risked mine shafts, dark and deep.
The plonk of a stone, dropped into water, far below.
Dad counted, One second, two, three… Four…ninety-two feet –
He grinned. Every second, it speeds up.
Kids drifted to sounds of the gold rush, pick and windlass.

But inside our classroom, we piloted Spitfires, strafing
Messerschmitt. A hit! The plane falling, aflame… Our teacher
paced, face aglow, afternoon classes recruited, into the battle.

Thrilling to the danger, of distant summer skies.
At three-thirty, older boys reminded Sir, Time
to go home. Surprise in our mentor's eyes.
His Spitfire hadn't even landed.

## Surge

Pan Demic is his name. We all retreat
from his game. No remorse for friend or foe,
this demon has far to go. He attacks strangers

day or night laughed in glee to see their plight,
flew first class by 747, or sailed on P&O. This deadly
dancer demonstrated his might, squeezing

breath from strong or meek and victims toppled
in the street. He watched the old gasp and weep,
suffocated the young and healthy too. There's

little intensive care could do. And while the globe
was on its knees, Pan Demic ignored our prayers
or pleas, killing pauper or king with delight. But

humans struggled on, a deadly fight. Red
our blood, dark the night. Numbers falling
in tangy waves of light. Pink seagull cries,

glimpse a rising in the skies. Bless the
missing, bless the sand, stepping into dawn.
Bless our tide, turning from its flood.

## Marking Time

My sister and I never got to say goodbye.
I hold the phone, a possum caught
in headlights.
My daughter says, Not Auntie Joan? A nod.
But, Mum, she was only thirty-nine.

You're forty.
What can I say? Sister. Best friend. She lit up my life.
ICU. Intubated. Unvisited.
A tug at my sleeve, But Mum, did Auntie know?
Gulp. Maybe, it was her time to go.
We couldn't attend the funeral.

Home schooling takes its toll. Struggling through my teacher role.
I sleep in my clothes. Forget to shower. Fighting to outpace
my demons. Faceless. Lurking in the dark. Haunting my days.
But smile, always smiles, for my girl.

Facebook message. I'm hoping an old friend
will get in touch. My words drop like stones,
joining others in the  lost river of life.

Days blur and muddle.
No sun or fresh air. Seven hundred new infections.
Covid death rates on the rise. Twenty-nine in local aged care.
My daughter crinkles her brow. Mum, are Gramps and Gran…?

I cross my fingers. Thank goodness, they're fine.
She snuggles closer. I miss them.
Me, too. But with borders closed…
A long look. And you, Mum?

Don't stress. We're safe in lockdown.
But if only there were some way to make that ache get lost.
She eyes my rumpled pyjamas. Mum, are you going to shower?
I'll choose your dress.
A laugh. You want me with make-up too… Why not?

## The Final Blow

You do what is needed to keep the ship on a
steady course. But proximity to a super sleaze
brings shivers of shame, a cabalist in his preferred

set of facts. You ask yourself how can I survive? You
compromise – there's too much at stake to leave.
Values you held dear under threat. You make a silent
vow to protect them now. A helpless fly bound by silken

threads. Convinced again, by odious conduct, not to go –
who else would preserve the status quo? You're too
important for the nation to lose. But in the final blow,

you find yourself using his words, praising his leadership
skills. Touting his commitment to low values. Failing the law,
another lost cog in the wheel. And your soul – swallowed whole.

# Approbium

I sent off my poor, imperfect baby, rich with nuance,
metaphor and symbol. Smarting, after Dad had declared, I don't
understand it at all. A story must have a beginning, middle and end.
I thought, you old bugger. After all my years of study,

you have the gall, to say this one fails the most basic test,
of the writing craft. Or was I onto something here?
Had he said it was good, could indicate a one-dimensional
tale. Me, I sought greater truths.

An existential take on difficult days, a family's exile, in
their own land. Driven to the unthinkable, by pride, failure
and distorted reality. But had my work,
captured the essence of this triple tragedy?

Seeking a verdict by editors who could only guess at my intentions,
and the dimensions of what I meant to say. Did this story,
like every poem, or work of art, whisper the truth, but
slant, and in a unique voice? My consolation prize,

praised my writing of the meal, a key scene,
one that summed up dissolution and desperation.
I cut, cut, cut. Wrote, rewrote, added, changed…
Had I achieved a more believable tone? It sped off again.

And Dad's scant regard for my work, galvanised me into
a rescue mission: three more of my tales languished in a drawer.
Excitement: two published, helpful comments on others.
And another couple would appear before long…

# Bal De Masque

Flirtation, laughter ,and Naro's glance lingers
on the décolleté
of my oyster silk chiffon. I blush like a teenager.
In a frisson of Scottish reels,

I'm stunned to hear his husky voice. I love you... A shaky
chuckle. Oh, my dear – it's the love of a boy for – for a woman
of an uncertain age...
Long hug. *Non, non, ma cherie*. I'm twenty...

My heart beats in overdrive. Quiver of the door keys
to his London pied à terre.
Goosebumps. The look in his eyes. His chuckles make me
tingle. And Japanese porcelain figures dance the Tango.

Bathrooms whisper of gold, orchids and marble.
A rose-scented soak. I buff my glowing skin, slipping into
a whisper of nightgown, silk.
Gasping when Naro appears, scarlet kimono unlocked.

We chuckle into one of the bedrooms. Wall mirrors, fragment
images of his tanned physique.
His tongue teases mine. Carved sandalwood bed.
Cherie, you won't need that. My nightie slides to the floor.
His robe drops on top.

In the scent of lilies, we can't seem to breathe.
The ache of sighs and giggles, skin to skin.
My petals quiver... Silent my plea, Don't wait.
Gosh! I'm awake. A Venetian mask covers my face.

## Black Lives

My friend bridles. Huh! All lives matter. Is she is being
deliberately obtuse? Should I add 'too' or 'do?'
She adds, I've blacks in my family. We had

indigenous girls in nursing school. Never
treated them any differently. US blacks
are lucky not to be back in Africa.

I feign agreement. How right you are. African Americans
must be grateful, living in the land of the free.
I'm sure George Floyd felt overjoyed to have such

good fortune. A cop's knee on his carotid, with hands
in pockets. The killer whistling, while his victim choked
to death…

## Crowned King

This new King of the Jews isn't Jewish,
but declares he's the chosen one. And if
people don't vote for him, they're disloyal.

Why, he's the most stable genius you've ever seen.
Yet folks act so mean. He offered to take Denmark's
Greenland off their hands. You'd think their PM

would seize his plan. Instead, she dismissed it as absurd –
a very nasty word, the worst insult you've ever heard.
He wanted to give himself a medal, musing it would be nice to

have one. But he wasn't allowed. Work? Think daily bullet points –
his minions say a page is as much as he can read – and that's a stretch.
Simple language is best. And they use his name a lot to keep him

on plot. But he seldom lasts as long as it takes. Drifting to matters
of his own devising. It's no longer surprising. And Potus insists his
crew hunt through papers each day for positive things people say.

It's seldom easy, and the way he gloats over crumbs of praise makes them
feel quite queasy. Fake news has gotten so bad he makes up his own
heroic deeds – bone spurs aside – the sort of copy he needs, Don't

blink at claims he helped rescuers at 9/11. Almost died in a helicopter
crash that killed a brace of his lackeys. And don't say it's tacky
the way he asserts doctors, gloved and gowned, left patients

in theatres, just to touch the hem of his sleeve. He has the strongest
economy ever seen, won the trade war with China. A coup, more
than others could do. Ranchers and farmers may not agree

but, really, he's the Best President the US has ever seen. Fit and ready to keep the job for life. And not about to let some God-awful bug, or Joe Biden's election win, bring strife. I won… Fraud… Litigation losses… I won't concede… And one fine day, all this will just go away

# Cool

Once a blade of shame cut self-esteem. Bearing the
curse of hand-me-down clothes. Poverty a cross
to bear making us aware of our humble position.

Taunts and blood, fist fights and scuffles.
Kids assessment right, pariahs in schoolyard
and street. Never guessing that frayed jeans

would become a fashion statement. More holes
than fabric, glimpses of knees, thighs or bum.
Another creation masquerades as a dress.

Torn black rectangles roughly stitched,
dangling by threads, with the air
of being salvaged from gran's ragbag.

## Dead Loss

Dieback affects valuable land. Loss of half
the pasture every year, costs farmers millions.
And not just in the north. It affects

tropical and subtropical buffle grass.
Yellows at the tips, and soon crushes into dust.
Acres of feed gone, or choked with weeds.

The Department of Agriculture refuses to believe
it's an issue. So the solution rests with property
owners. They ask, too much fertiliser? A fungus?

Research needs money, and fast. It hit hard
six years ago, on fertilised and unfertilised
land. They tried burning, plowing, re-sowing.

Nothing worked. Suspicion fell on the mealy
bug. They hide in deep soil, fluffy white.
One asks, does their toxic saliva and sticky

residue kill the grass? They irritate the skin, too.
Some say to plant legumes and forest crops –

not tasty to the bug. With mental health
and money at risk, farmers can't afford
to bide their time. Ready to do anything.

# Fickle Beasts

At storm's edge, a snail trailed a silver path
of division.
We'd trodden these shells of misunderstanding

for decades. It didn't do to challenge her bleak
take on childhood. She corrected any positive
interpretation of mum, dad, friends and lovers.

But I remember, she cries. Dare I tell her that
memories are fickle beasts? They trick us into
believing what never happened. Denying what did.

It escalates into shouts. She throws up her
hands and does a runner.
I take up my pen…

## Glacial

Scent of lilies. His pain over, mine just begun.
I caressed those stilled hands.
Gifted. Loving. Pallid…
Kissed his waxen brow.

A blink away from the dying sun,
the ignition key trembled.
I half-expected to waken,
clasped in his arms. Soothing
me back to life. But, adrift, on the mourning air,

his voice echoed. The heavy silence of bookshelves,
and model trains. Our deserted house ticked away
lonely hours, as if nothing had changed,
But I flinched from the glacial steppes,
of our marital bed.

# Grand Dame

I'm sad to farewell this grand old dame.
Global traveller, host to millions.
Queen of the skies.
Jumbo of the thermals.
With all the grace of a kangaroo,
you flew, for almost fifty years.
Performed Darwin Cyclone rescues –
and others, too

You took the prize for size, range and reliability.
Well ahead of your time, capable and strong,
with Cut-price World travel. You escorted Fred, Jed,
and Great-aunt Rose. Wings of freedom,
and wonders to behold.

Your final lap of honour, off the Australian coast.
You sketched the flying kangaroo,
in white,
before floating away to retirement.
Resting, on the warm desert sands of Mojave.

# Hunkered Down

All bets were off when humans left town. Some hunkered down
in homes and apartments, to simmer out isolation.
Bears, goats and monkeys wandered empty streets.
Enjoying a treat: to experiment and eat garden plants.

While some took a fun run on empty roads, cars hibernated
out of sight. In the quicksands of time and 2020 Covid, we heard
the chirp of birds, long gone from crowded streets. And planes
with wings clipped, allowed our planet to breathe fresh air.

Indians admired the distant Himalayas, clear of fog, for the first
time in years. And the Chinese wiped tears, relishing the sudden
break from the dark breath of industry.
Walking the Great Wall, smog free, they could see the
wonders of every brick and tree, under naked skies.

## Invasion

Private jets, BMWs and Mercedes,
fled a deadly foe. New York, London,
and Connecticut, too, ticketed to go. They
invaded small communities, with zero hospital
beds or ventilators. Holed-up with

their sense of entitlement.
Locals signed petitions to keep the strangers out. Closed bridges
to fake tans and diamonds. One gold bracelet brought
her own ventilator, gowns and PPEs.

But angry locals, surviving from one paycheque
to the next,
or taking community handouts,
grudged them service.

Some intruders annexed rooms at night,
fearing boil-overs from residents.
They stormed into zones, of holiday homes,
confident of being safe.

But an invisible foe
floated from coughs and sneezes,
carrying high virus loads. Wafting,
unremarked, on country breezes.

# Isolation

Guilt and shame made me falter my name. A nurse –
what was I doing infected? Hated the thought
of leaving my lovely patients.
And welcomed the support from other nurses

all afflicted with Covid-19, despite our precautions.
Out of breath, cough, wellness checks…
We juggled calls from colleagues and friends,
those still on the front line. Three times a day,

masked and gowned, staff left me a meal tray.
Was it food or cardboard?
A virtual birthday cake. Alone, a mum in isolation,
I'm desperate for a hug. My son texted me

links to YouTube music. On Skype, I shivered
at a strange conversation.
My kids debated the merits of having
a Corona infection, so they might join me.

Nurses mourned colleagues who had died. Petrified
at the thought we might not survive. Our poor kids…
And some folk had won the fight for life,
but lost the will to live.

# Mission Accomplished

We dance, mutate and celebrate: another perfect host.
The old make easy prey, we watch them gasp
and slip away. And our kind are not averse

to the odd doctor or nurse, regardless of their ages.
But while the populace weeps and rages, the death
toll turns, a thousand pages. We catch the young
while on the run, target bathers soaking sun.

Here's to a babe in its mother's arms. He takes no solace
from our charms. We proliferate in lungs, leak bodily
juices, giving neither apology nor excuses. It's strike,
strike and strike again. Attacking gaps in mask, gown
or gloves, we seize our chances.

The target's cells weep blood, and slowly die.
Our deadly dancers sigh and shrivel, too. But that's
what we were born to do. Others soon will take
our places. Embracing all the creeds and races.

## No Visitor Allowed

Slurred glass panel high in my door
I'm woken, gasping for air. A house brick on my chest.
Demons dance a hobnailed tango, on my brow.
Doctors and nurses confer, outside my door. Should it be the ICU?
Monitor her in my ward, for now. A glimmer of morning light.
I'm less distressed, but far from well. Masked and gowned,
a nurse enters my cell. I wear a mask. Another swab test.

Resolve and fear in his eyes. Cotton bud stuck up my nose
and throat. I gag, cough and vow not to cry. It must be done.
But why at 5 a.m.? He leaves me a dish of warm water. No time
to chat and share my day. I sponge myself. The kitchen girl
leaves my tray, and hurries away. I miss my sense of taste
and smell. Doctors and nurses consult outside. Obs OK. Oxygen
levels drop when she's asleep. Another X-ray on the way.

More tests every day. The needle pierces my vein, she
releases the tourniquet. Blood fills a tube. You're looking
better. Her words surge with warmth. But Covid-19 plays
by its own rules. About to go home, when it creeps back.
A waiting game. The latest checks. The next meal.
Will this dread disease ever set me free?

## No Case For Race

My parents arrived from Malaysia. Beguiled to find
friendly Aussies. I'm born here, the sunny coast
my home. Before this Covid war, strangers waved

and smiled. But under siege from this silent foe,
people I've known for years, pivot, and go. Some
give me odd looks. While an oldie shouts, Where's

your mask? Well he might ask: he doesn't wear one.
Outside a fish shop, a chap raises sudden fears. He's
face to face, invading my social space.

Effing Chinese bitch! Go home. We don't
want you here. He spits.
I wipe my cheek.
An outrage away from tears.

## Chaos

Renovations taking place. Supports shake,
slide, fall… A voice says they shouldn't
have continued building, with fire still alight,
underground. Smoke swirls and billows,

I organise an evacuation. Contact the police.
Find Matron's number. Smoke issues
from the phone. The kitchen ablaze.
Ambulance, police and fire brigade sirens

wail and resonate. The walking evacuated first.
Often wondered how I'd react, in a crisis. Acrid
smoke, fireman fight the blaze. A chaos of confused
residents, shaky planks, and plaintive cries.

Where am I? Want my bed. Cough. The SES demand
the files to write their reports. Papers splash
into water, sodden in seconds. Ambulance officers
rush out the bed-bound, police join the fray. After all

this effort will I be get a medal? And where are the time
sheets? Surely they'll pay me the extra hours? Miffed,
I haven't received any pay for ages… But what's that?
Our Siamese cat kneading away my nocturnal adventures.

## Party Perennial

I've kissed a princess, shaken hands with a PM.
While a president, or two, are on my list. I've sipped
champers at weddings, and celebration dinners for three.
Climbed the Duomo and St Pauls too. I do what I have to –
a party perennial, that's me.

I may be small and invisible, but size isn't all. I hitch rides
on rickshaws, 747s and cruise liners as well. I've travelled
first class from Wuhan, to Lombardy, New York
and Sydney, too. And it's you who pay –
a party perennial, that's me.

Calls to demonstrate, stop isolation, are what I like to hear.
The yips and yells, their raucous cheers, are magic to my ears. I love
the way they mix, and mingle. It's the perfect spot. I infect the lot.
Invade throat or lung, whether old or young. A spike in numbers.
That's the way it has to be. But when the siren's wail ends their
tale, I step aside. A party perennial? Don't blame me.

# Pandemic

i

Stirring among a wok people,
these Smallsters were Not for Sale.
But they hitched rides
on rich and poor.

ii

Invisible,
dancing their way from human,
to human.
Shaking hands with dukes and earls. Cuddled
up to strings of pearls.

iii

Travelled first class on planes
and ships.
Sailed on holiday cruises.
Blossomed from hugs and sneezes.

iv

Sparkled in cough droplets ,on breezes.
Floated on air, alive for hours.
Invaded mouth, nose and lungs.
Slight cough, breathless…

v

The demons stormed cells,
multiplied, mutated.
Patients sick so darned quick.
Respirators breathing by the score.

vi

Victims Isolated in ICU.
Steroids, IV.
Another loss –
Corona's Pyrrhic victory.

vii

Long-haulers short of breath.
Foggy thinking, hair loss,
fatigue.
Hallucinations.

viii

And think crazy dreams,
growl of lions, tigers, monkeys.
And, after weeks on a ventilator,
your mouth too sore to drink.

## Revelation

It was ages since we'd met. Maybe
counselling and hypnosis had brought
peace and harmony?

But her hugs morphed into fantasy.
Flint-edged words cut me,
one by one, dripping blood.

I reeled from her dark place,
shocked and outraged.
No, Lal. That never happened

I remember it well…

I took a deep breath.
No, Lal…

But I was there. I saw you… Him too…

What else lurked in her grimy little mind?
Believe me, you're wrong…

Creased brow. You're in denial. Do you think I'm mad?

## Stay at Home

Lockdown rules flaunted, by those who'd tested positive.
One in four break the edicts. Pub crawl by one bloke spread the virus.
And self-styled libertarians object to mask-wearing, on spurious

ideological grounds. Young policewoman assaulted by
one of them, female, who thinks the world is all
about her. No concern for infection, contamination,
or likely deaths. There's heavy fines for sneaking over

closed borders, without a permit. Even so some
give it a go. And bosses with no sense of community,
insist workers turn up to their post, even those with coughs and.
sneezes. Insecure, casual and poorly paid jobs pose a dilemma.
Should they work and ensure their family eat –
or play by Covid mandates?

## Shrine

A would-be dictator lies in or out of his bunker. Hiding
behind a make-do wall. Shrine, for protestors posters,
and lives taken. Hearts mourn, dignity shaken. Children

caged, lives broken. Birthday balloons, souls
of hope, break free, floating sky-high. We march
arm-in-arm, black and white, justice for all. Tread

no more paths of anguish and pain. Cease all
uniformed violence. Deaths in custody, writ large, in
yellow paint. I can't breathe resonates around the

globe. Streets of New York, Washington, and Sydney
shout, enough. Dry-eyed for Bristol's slave-trader's
statue. Toppled, into a watery grave.

# Snagged

We trod the dusty path home from school, mottled
with casuarina shadows. Gurgling ripples gave way
to deep pools, my brother skipping stones.

Khaki Campbell ducks brought chuckles.
Tipping back their heads, water dripped
from beaks, filtered, from their prey.

One day at the brook, a back-cast. The hook snagged
our friend in the base of his thumb. Dad frowned.
*Reckon you could hold still, while I open it up a bit?*

Robin nodded, gritting his teeth. At nine he didn't
utter a sound, while Daddy's sharpest
pocket knife cut into flesh.

Blood flowed.
Brave lad, well, done. It's out.

## You'll Be Safe

Far from New Year's Eve city rainbows of glitter
and the joyous birth of 2020, a high school hall
crouches in darkness. Safe for now. Hundreds
huddle, choking on acrid smoke. Children whimper,
oldies snore on floors. Parents rigid with fright. But
a pair of orange overalls gives advice. Join our convoy,
leaving soon – there's no guarantee you'll be safe. Take

enough fuel for an hour's drive, to the next town. And
please write down your names on this Coroner's list –
should things go amiss. A honeymoon pair hold hands
and ponder should they wait and see? Nobody can say
if it will be better here – or there. Dread grows. To stay
or go? A day earlier it was safe at the creek. Then sirens

screamed, lights flashed blue and red. The monster
roared like a jumbo jet but a local pub was safe –
until it wasn't. And they were absolutely fine in
the scout hall. Low on water, out of power, encircled
by flames. Told it might be wise to leave. Should they
stake their lives on a risky drive through a charred
landscape? Morning dark as night, edged by a reddish
glow. Hearts heavy, they left. Dozens of trucks, four-
wheel drives and cars, escorted along the deserted

highway. The saddest drive of their lives. Native fauna
in charred piles. Screams from the dying. Trees
aflame both sides of the road, knuckles white on
steering wheels. Houses explode. Scorched carcasses
of dead cows and kangaroo. Two homes saved, a miracle
glimpsed in a desert of blackened earth and twisted metal.
A small town evacuated the previous night, now their own
desperate flight, along a fire-impacted road the last thing
crisis crew want to do but it's a new normal –
to this climate change emergency.

## The Art of Survival

Humans learn the art of survival from birth,
on an earth that wobbles out of control
with one slip of the dice. Contagion woes,
car crashes, a tussle with a shark…

But whites rarely experience racial slurs.
Rarely get shot in the back, unless
they're dealing ice.
Anglo-Saxon heritage, folk seldom suffer
unlawful arrest, or deaths in custody.
People of colour endure such abuse every day.

They drill their kids on ways to survive.
Be invisible. Don't answer back, even if the cop is wrong.
Stopped in your car? Keep your hands on the wheel.
No hoodies. Never argue with a white. Keep car radio down –
Blacks are shot for loud music. Shot reaching to the glovebox,
for their license. 'Illegal' US kids, Latin-American babies to teens,
are locked in cages. Lost to parents. Deported alone, to lands
they've never known.
By a Statue of Liberty country, founded on free immigration.

## The Chunnel

Two drilling teams planned to meet halfway, under
the roiling English channel, La Manche. But, Mon Dieu,
suppose the French crew took theirs in one direction,
and the Brits in another – and one tunnel missed
the other, perhaps by hundreds of metres? Laser
beam technology to the rescue. Brit alignment
began on the English shore, guiding a control panel
button, ceaselessly adjusted. A drill tore through
carbonate. In their wake, tons of material spewed
forth, and at a fast rate. But where could it go? The
populace said no to piles of spoil, marring the green

fields of Kent. Let waste be transformed into an asset.
Extend space at the base of the Shakespeare Cliffs.
Double steel walls, with concrete poured in between.
Dividers to consolidate over four million tons of chalk
marl. Sea water yielded, thirty hectares of land snitched
from the channel, hitched to the Dover cliffs. Samphire
Hoe Park, lush pasture for cattle and sheep. Tool storage
work material building lot, and the largest cooling system
in Europe. Intercountry train carriages must be kept

comfortable at below thirty degrees. But rail tunnel
drilling sloshed to a sudden halt. Floods of water rose
to men's knees. Pump-out failed to slow the flow.
How to avert disaster, should it be the trickle
from tons of ocean water above? A taste-test. Fresh water.
Aeons trapped in the carbonate, suddenly gushing free.
Epoxy injections sealed the fractured chalk. Lost time
sped into additional crew. Target met, joyous breakthrough.
Brits had breached the French Service Tunnel. April 1994.

The best French champagne bubbled, toasting a tunnel error of only 3.5 cm. Cheers. Glasses clinked. They nibbled canapes. Brit and Gaelic hugs. Then the French broke through the main tunnel. But alcohol banned! Gaelic lads lucky to enjoy a glass of lukewarm water. Eurotunnel. Grand opening day on 6 May 1994 celebrated by the Queen and France's president, François Mitterrand. The Chunnel, 50.45 kilometres from Dover to Calais. Hip, hip, hooray. Longest railway tunnel in the world.

## The Next Battle

Gowned. Masked. Gloved.
The excitement and adrenalin rush
rapidly overwhelmed
by the magnitude of patients with tubes.
The hum and shush of machines.
Yell. Hand hygiene. Sanitise.
Beep. Beep. Beep.

Patients deteriorate after only hours
struggling for breath. Lung lining hardens.
The sickest know their fate. Nurses see it
in frightened eyes.
Battling their own fears.
Will they catch it too?

Two weeks on ventilators. Patients die alone.
No relative's hug. No priest to pray.
Staff long to do more.
Struggling to keep grief at bay.
Exhausted by numbers.
While army trucks haul coffins
to pop-up morgues.

An entire generation lost.
Only in the privacy of their rooms
dare nurses allow themselves to weep.
Weep for all the patients lost that day.
Fatigue drives their sleep. Stalks every shift.
Waking in darkness, they don their armour.
Another battle in this Corona war.

## Wily Lady

The tide had turned. Deaths dropped. Shock-jocks
quickly deemed our shutdown wasted time and money.
Each sideshow ignoramus flayed the airwaves, ignoring

how self-isolation and sacrifice kept the plague's tally down. Chuckle
at this band, for calling Australia's victory a failure. But never
underestimate this deadly lady. Relief sighed into dismay the day

she joined mates congregated at their local, newly-open.
And then slipped between a standards glitch in lockdown.
Minders masks on, gloves on – and that was it. Touching, hugs.

Nobody imposed social distance. They made it easy.
She took a stretch from school to housing estate, people
with symptoms ignored their disease, taking a state back to its

knees and, by degrees, we saw the numbers rise and rise.
Borders closed, new rules imposed, masks mandated.
Should we have forged ahead with our freedoms – or waited?

# Undulate

The northern lights undulate
In green
Above jagged peaks
Iced in white
Dark sky dripping stars
Until golden streaks
Stretch towards a field
And elongated shadows of horses
Trot into morning

## Fall

In the beech forest, I pitched
forward, spreadeagled on glass.
A sliver attacked my hand.

Entry and exit wound,
on my little finger,
flushing red.

Shaken, I rose. Figuring recent
rain, had left the weapon
clean. And bugs likely to have been

expelled, by the red river of my blood.

## Humble Pie

Suddenly awake, I struggle to escape the grip
of a nightmare. Terrified to discover the upper part
of my body paralysed. I try to scream, but my lips

are frozen, too, except for the right corner. Gordon
doesn't heed my strangled cries. The lower part
of my body isn't locked. I bump him with my bum.

He fails to stir. Another muffled cry. At my point
of desperation, he hugs me. Darling, what's up?
Movement floods back. Arm muscles ache.

Pins and needles in my hands. Gordon switches
on the light and gets a fright. Why, you're trembling
all over. I swallow humble pie. Months ago, I dismissed

your experience as a bad dream…

## I am Lived

Touch the whole truth, if you can agree what it is. Life happens
when you aren't looking. Some say it is, what you think it isn't.
Shift your vision. Don't settle for alternate reality. Sometimes

you only know things were there, when they aren't. Seek
paths you never knew existed. Beware lions, tigers and blue
tongue lizards. Fly with angels. But accept reality when

you can't browbeat it into silence. Things must change
to stay the same. I am lived by unexpected events.
But don't become a passive measure of your life.

You'll struggle, sacrifice, hurt, in the brief interval
between life and death. Do what good you can. Respect
your fellow humans, regardless of colour, race or creed.

But when the road ahead is shorter than the one behind,
keep your options open. Seek answers. Expect miracles.
And isn't this a delightful, introspective sauvignon blanc?

## Memories

A childhood gazing through plate glass. Isolated
from my peers, during those formative years. Only
one friend, my sister, two against the world.

I pondered the mystery of how acquaintance
bloomed into friendship – or love. Adolescence,
everything out of kilter. Tall when others were

short. Hiding my size ten feet under chairs, hoping
nobody would notice. A snigger. You have a good
grip on Australia. Cheeks aflame. The fear of not

recognising someone, met a second time.
The effort it took to enter a crowded room,
one shoulder lower than the other…
Would everybody notice and laugh?

## Trump

I couldn't possibly agree with you.
Then we'd both be wrong.
And I'm sure that God has better

things to do than bless a loser.
Like that chump in the White House.
But don't think Potus is being naïve,

or stupid, in spruiking this drug.
Forget treating the sick and dying –
hospital ventilators and all that.

He's preparing for a killing
on those shares.
Millions of doses ready to roll.

## Losses

In the foreplay to a long life, I lived the joy
of all my senses. Guessing one day the glory
of sight would fade into the call for spectacles.

My hair took on grey shades one day, restored
to a blonde hue, one I never knew. Age spots
are my due, wrinkles too. One or two teeth

went missing – though I never knew that words,
once heard with clarity, would get up and go.
Voices tease, in a monotone of sounds, lacking

substance or meaning. Missing half the
conversation has become my norm.
Hearing what wasn't said but not

what is. Laughter is my weapon of choice,
to alleviate the weight of loss and frustration.
I call on experts to adjust my ailing aids,

## Freedom

Paul a kid in care. One teacher stole a frizzy lock
of his hair. You're my cuddly panda. Another declared,
I could eat you up. The five-year-old leapt out of reach,
trembling. I know why I've never met another black boy…

In the years of his majority, Paul's skin marked the
colour of disdain. Lumped in, as kin ,with a
discordance of fear, from the Caribbean. Outsider.
The sting of perfect accent and superb English,
seeking his birthright: equality in British society.

He tackled the Omnibus Union's ban on black, brown
or Asian drivers. Dubbed, dishonest and irresponsible.
Awarded five hundred pounds, in damages. De trop in
working men's clubs. Ousted from a pub: given your hue
we've no need of you. Eight hours locked in a Bristol jail.
Eight cops different versions of Paul's arrest that night

His plight negated, evidence from an Irish chap,
pub witness. Paul's redress, twenty-five quid.
But watch the river of life flow on and on…
Greet the first, black youth worker, in town.
And salute the first black man
accorded Freedom of Bristol City.

## Solo

Pallid and thin, he rested on a sun lounge.
Blessed by a jacaranda dance of violet bells. They
chimed hope. It broke her heart, knowing… Every day

they trod its carpet, deep with memories and dreams.
His passing, at only fifty-five, left her only half-alive.
She plummeted into a different world – a haven

for couples. Shocked, she hadn't noticed it before.
Old and young, hand-in-hand they strolled the
streets. Lingered over coffee and tea. At thirty

with eligible chaps by the score, she may
have found another man. By fifty or more,
numbers dwindled. Failed hearts, strokes,

or men who decided they preferred blokes.
Many sought firm flesh to boost floppy – egos.
Started second families.
While she swallowed HRT, planning exotic trips –
solo.

## Santorini

I set my alarm for break of day at Santorini bay, site
of an ancient volcano. Our ship lay in wait for first light.
I make a foray from my cabin, camera at the ready.

Decks are slippery and wet from the spray. Moisture drops
mottle the white railing. The seascape is stolen by a fog.
Morning sky and sun missing too. I quell disappointment.

Yearning for ghostly glimpses of jagged cliffs. About
to stash my Minolta, when a Japanese lass floats
to the rail. A waterfall of black hair, decorated by

a big yellow bow. Tresses flow below her cream cardigan. She's tiny.
Long, floral skirt, in hues of orange and blue, matching sneakers.
I sense both her excitement and gloom over the mystery – a hidden
arrival. I press the button. Hurray! A perfect shot.

## Philosophers

Plato and early Greek philosophers took the notion
of the recovery seriously. Thousands at the brink,
floated into a different consciousness, with no word for death.
A dream state but not a dream.
Death is the dream. Plato's dialogue, Socrates dying.

I withdrew from my body. Hyper-reality. Brilliant life-light, profound love. Peace beyond my imagination. Spirit forms of loved ones, helped folk through the transition into another realm of existence. Timeless. A panorama of every action I'd ever done, unfolded one by one. Kind or unkind. But this time, I heard them from the perception of the wounded. Experiences arrived in sequence. Learning is life, the quest for knowledge eternal…

Many told to go back. I was given a choice. My NDE released me from the fear of death. The afterlife is not a scientific but philosophic question, Plato took it at face value. A continuum from the solidity of our bodies to a miracle – eternity.

## Omniscient

Dew-laden breeze. We scaled steep flanks, groping
for handholds.
Climbed higher, inch by inch, edging towards the sky.
In the broil of noon, muscles screamed, but we plodded on.
Hitchhikers crawled and tickled.
I grabbed a leafy switch, whipping away the pests.

Kurragong tree comfort, dripping white bells. A shade-caressed
break for corned-beef sandwiches and tea.
Far below, a cloud of dust urged me home.
My sister shook her curls. You want to give up?
Never!
Shale pinged from sneaker-clad feet.

The summit perspired. Shimmered. Close,
but never any closer. One foot… After… Another…
Stunted trees gasped for breath. The stink of dogwood
scorned scratched hands.
Would I ever reach the top?

One blink later, we stepped onto the plateau. Trig station welcome
A willy-wagtail danced our sarabande of victory. Blue and mauve
hills nestled in the palm of victory. Glisters of a gold, flashed from
an afternoon river. Distant farmsteads. Shadows crept towards
the wonder of another moonlit night.

## Puy de Fou

A broken castle roars with flames, reflected in the lake.
Gipsy girls dance flamenco on water. Applause roars and ripples,
huddled under brollies. Mirrored steeds tinkle, spinning on
a carrousel. Haystacks giggle and sneeze, while cavorting
lovers romp, and geese parade in a tail-wiggle formation.

The thunder of hooves, chariot races, and Roman gladiators. King Arthur
clashes swords, with lace and ostrich feathers on hats. Gold and blue
caparisons, for horses, coursers and rounceys. They trot the melting stage,
in a son et lumière, frolic through the ages, a seven-hundred-year history,
at la Vendée, in the Loire. But revolution and war stains the musket

and cannon-blasted pages. While flashes of brilliant light, captivate,
a bruine-sprinkled night of transcendence. But memory
and reality pirouette, hand-in-hand, with myth and legend.
A spell exploding, into farewell stars and colour, in flight.

# Odyssey

Too many tongues have teased and torn at the threads
of Joseph's past, attempting to unravel the truth. A truth
made dim by the misty paths of conjecture and time. The
journey of Odysseus lasted ten years. This one has travelled
on for nigh two hundred. Dare we seek to speak of Great-grandpa's
battles with mythical beasts, lost in the twists of winding paths?
Friend to a bushranger, he said, *they made him what he was.*

Pickaxe and shovel marked his way, gilded by nuggets of gold.
Walk now the blurred by-ways, charmed by his derring-do,
warming the pages of an unwritten family history. Blood
dripped onto the stone of honour. His sea voyage flight
far from the badge of injustice. A tall, handsome man.
But were his wary eyes, those of a convict? Three men
in Van Diemen's Land bore his name. None came to our

colony at the right time. Did he skip a ship at Port Melbourne?
Change names and dates, making his adventures a mystery,
his history told and retold. Variations at each telling blurred
the past. Too many campfire stories have blazed and died, ashes
never divined. Details a tangle of vines and brambles, concealing
the real Joseph. Tom or Jed. Tales of a brother at Ballarat
goldfields, begging him to face the staff of justice in California.

Hear the creak of windlass at Gulgong. There he married a girl
half his age, dressed in black. Rivers flowed, muddied from
too many dishes swirling for gold. Too many failed shafts
driven into hard Australian earth, for us to find pay dirt?

## New World View

The German romantic poet Holderlin
says that poetry is not a luxury but the core to dwelling,
of being. Billy Collins, US Poet Laureate and White House

poetry reader for a president, declares a poem a day is
the way to go bringing this treasure-house of wonder
and delight to the daily routine. Certainly he would not

express his sentiments like mine. He inhabits a modern
world where conversational tone takes the words close
to those one might share on the phone. Laid-back, though
still the best words in their best order, bringing a sense

of delight to what, for others, might be rendered banal.
Fully occupy a place, find a gut-level connection. Why do whites
seek to dominate their space, instead of being as one with the land?

We ignore the cries for help of this great continent at your
peril. Let's preserve its many wonders, learn to listen,
take the next steps towards healing. Too often we

pollute with gas, coal and oil for profit, ignoring the treasures
of history and humanity, written in bones beneath our feet.
Huge mines bring spoil. Environment and heritage sold to

the highest bidder. Blown up for another mine, while politicians
tell us all will be fine. Do you sit in architectural boxes, piled high
in the sky, one upon another? Or trapped by large homes that
imprison, rather than connect. Counting your wealth, but

forgetting humanity's place in the life cycle of the earth?
Struggling through death tolls and loved ones lost. This
lockdown feels a living hell, cowering behind the walls we dwell.
Perhaps social distancing will see the demise of high rise.

A city of strangers, in a world mortally wounded by an invisible
foe. Add climate change, drought, fire and flood. Not a breath
of fresh air. Our cells boast air con, oxygen recycled. Infection,

spread by social attitudes and behaviour. Urban sprawl,
infrastructure expense, loss of fertile land for food.
And habitat destruction – animals driven to extinction.

# Immortality

Physicians said, My God, he's dead. But, I'd never felt so alive.
Watching the resuscitation of my physical body, I heard
their speech and thoughts. But they couldn't hear me.
I floated in a new consciousness, a place with no death.
A dream state, but not a dream. Plato and early Greek
philosophers took NDEs seriously, exploring the notion
of recovery, a transition into another realm of existence.

It's not a scientific but philosophic question. Plato took
knowledge as infinite. A continuum, from the solid object
of our bodies, to the miracle of eternity.
Medical societies study near death experiences. Their mystery
and majesty changes lives. But never try to persuade others.
They must find their own enlightenment.

In Plato's dialogues, Socrates is dying. I withdrew from my body
into a hyper-reality of brilliant light, and profound love...
It brought me tranquillity. Spirit forms of loved ones hover,
helping mortals through the transition to eternity. A panorama
shows every day of our existence. We learn compassion,

listening to others from the perspective of the wounded.
My less pleasant actions and attitudes filled me with shame.
Some folk were told to return to their bodies. Others, like me,
given a choice. I came back for my children and wife.
The miracle of life heightened, by the wonder of my NDE.
At peace, freed from the dread of death.

## Defiance

In the bluish haze of this arid valley, we navigate steep
cuttings, bump over corrugations, ebonised trunks
of eucalyptus stand defiant. Not a leaf stirs in the acrid air.

Hills black with soot, and in the half-burnt field of a farm lost
to weeds, not a tuft of grass. Ribbed stock huddle awaiting
the next handout. At a household water tank, one calloused hand

taps rungs. and his battered Akubra scans smoky skies. Dust spirals
in our wake. A rumble of cattle grids mark the rutted road
on our right a watercourse of stones and boulders baking in the

midday sun. Sporadic pools of brown water bring a hint of green,
picking at their edges. I recall the burble of a crystal brook,
family picnics, and billy tea shared under whispering casuarinas.

We splashed and swam in rippling delight, fished for yabbies,
eels and gudgeons. I glimpse the windows of our old house,
blinded by cobwebs. Its sagging skeleton leans against

a lemon tree heavy with fruit. Here my old school gate
squeaks. Paint peels. No tang of chalk or childrens'
chatter, only the scuttle of disappearing mice.

Outside, the stink of roadkill. A squirrel glider, its fluffy tail
singed, susceptible like all creatures on this earth
to the ravages of climate change and wheels of chance.

## Strut and Crow

Bridge-building equipment, double-size.
Traffic crawls and grumbles. Police cars and
Council escorts, lights blink and circle,
edging their obstacle along the road.

Stock and Station Agent Dunnedoo. Café tea for
two. And a lady, born here. Married here.
Divorced here. Lived here all my life. A laugh.
Why, you're almost a local.

Cumulus shadows mottle tufted hills.
A line of white letterboxes, one red,
chat to a queue of dams, flowing downhill.
Emu sighting at Tooraweenah, lost at speed.

I friend I knew once lived nearby. I pictured
standing in the pub, asking after her family.
But the road had other ideas.

## A Breath of Covid

Keep a social distance. Visualise your alveoli,
absorbing oxygen into the blood,
host to microbial life forms, bacteria, and viruses.
This normal human exchange with lung and atmosphere,
begins at birth. But in 2020, a deadly foe switched
the web of life to danger zone, risking our lives on earth.
Some folk bare-faced, take shallow breaths in public.
Flinch at other people's coughs. Afraid of Covid
aerosols, floating on the air. In these pandemic days,
exhalations may be lethal.

Masks a physical and moral necessity. Lockdown, in extremis,
a mutual responsibility, stopping transmissions and helping
save lives. A small act of collective power and solidarity.
Online and internationally we take care, sharing survival
strategies and information, until we get a vaccine.
Physically separated, but not isolated, screens bring Celtic
relaxation music, Zoom, online concerts.
And Duolingo, to sparkle up your French.

## Indigenous

Parishioners led hunting parties after church, shooting
tribes at will. Men burned down blacks' circular homes,
on their own land, lately dispossessed.
Poisoned wells, crimes to conceal reality. Pioneers dogged
in the belief of white superiority. But explorers used
warriors knowledge of water sources, for desert survival.

Colonial settlers' granted indigenous land, stole black
house slaves. Cattle-yard slaves. Money seldom seen.
They borrowed convict slaves, to clear ill-gotten acres.
Kidnapped South Sea Islanders, sugar-cane slaves…
No slavery in Australia?

Shadows whisper of past wrongs. Sorry began this
crucial journey.
But we haven't yet stopped, to respect the Uluru
statement. step forward in unison, find dignity
and empathy. Kin under the colour of our skin.

## Nobody in Charge

All regular staff away. Some had Covid-19.
More than fifty residents infected.
Close contacts sent home.

The place run by a nurse-in-training,
and one care assistant.
A rush of showers, feeding, dressing…
Residents fed breakfast late. Admin staff dispensed meds.

One resident on IV fluids. A very sick lady gasped,
I can't breathe, give me air. Oxygen helped.
Told the young doctor, she needs hospital care.
He wouldn't meet my eyes. My boss says she stays here.

Nobody in charge of PPEs. Inferior masks.
Rubbish spilt on the ground. Oops,
cross-contamination.

On the twelve-hour shift I comforted families –
over the phone. No visitors allowed. Days later
my positive Covid test.
Had the mouthpiece been sanitised?

# Masked

How dare you demand I wear a mask. My civil
rights are all I ask. Force me to do so and I'll sue.
What else is a citizen to do?

Soon she coughs and sneezes –
aerosols float, on gentle breezes. She infects young
and old, thinks it's just a heavy cold. Hospitals

treat victims by the score, while Covid-19 hunts
for more. Patients gasp for breath, another dies
Nurses shiver at their cries. But don't succumb to whims
and fancies. Wear a mask and help your chances.

## Toppled

A would-be dictator lies in his bunker
behind a pop-up wall. On the wires of his
invention, protestors hang artworks. This

make-do gallery welcomes messages profound.
Traces dignity lost, not found. Birthday greetings
to the fallen. Arm-in-arm, black or white, we seize

the fight, craving miracles. A wall weeps
for black lives taken. Aches for generations
of pain and suffering I can't breathe resonates

around the globe. Life kneed out, on his carotid.
In streets of Washington, and Sydney feet speak out.
In Bristol slave-trade statue toppled. Watery grave.

## Game of Cards

Happy birthday, son.
Imagine! Three years old…

Enjoying post-party fun, parents take a turn
at the table.
Adult friends laugh at the Joker
and each other. Men clink glasses of whisky.
The ladies sip champagne.
They all ignore the clock‘s warning.
Tick tock.

One man sings and jests like a king.
The winner slaps down an ace
of spades. And fails to notice,
a loss from his pocket…
Tick tock.

But the prowling boy, on the floor
finds a prize by the door. Nobody guesses
he's about to play his final score.
Triggered, by a chance discovery.
Tick tock.

Bang! Red spreads and ebbs from his chest.
Cards scatter. Chairs overturn. Shouts. Call 911
No pulse. No breath.
Mother wails, Nooo! My boy, my little boy…
Father yells, This ain't no frontier war.
How many more innocent kids have to die?

## Catastrophic

The city shook and roared. People fled, treading
carpets of glass. Earthquake fear.
Choking on black smoke, acrid smell.
Shock wave of death and destruction,
ambulance sirens. Cars covered in dust,
overturned. Headlights ablaze, horns blared.

Une ville of shattered bricks, twisted metal
and broken bodies.
People swore they saw more damage, than in the civil war.
Hundreds of thousands roamed the streets, looking for
places to sleep. Silo of wheat destroyed.
What might the populace eat?

Covid-overwhelmed hospitals shattered.
Patients evacuated.
Faces dripped red. A pharmacist plucked glass
slivers from cheeks. Disinfected wounds, bandaged limbs…
and still the line of wounded wound on.

Dogs sniffed, indicating the buried. Rescuers scrabbled
with bare hands and shovels. Relatives keened
and wept. Truth filtered through, to shouts of dismay.
Ammonium nitrate explosion. Port warehouse. Anger
escalated into disarray. What sort of government
stored tons of dangerous chemicals at the centre of Beirut –
and for years?

## Zapped

A lightning bolt zigzagged through me
my body supine on the ground,
a nurse, doing CPR.
Friends' shocked voices.
Eyes focused on me, the victim.

But I'm here, over the way. Separate. Watching.
I make to tap a friend's shoulder, saying, that's me. Spooked
when my hand goes straight through. Surprised he doesn't
know I'm there. Drifting, I see the foggy image,
of my legs, shimmer,
and disappear.

I pass through a wall. My wife is reading to our
grandson. Giggling over the story fun.
Bluish light shines all around me,
clear and bright. But they don't notice I'm there.

I float into a new dimension of reality,
dream-like, but not a dream.
Suffused with pure love and energy, attached
to everything. My universal questions answered, one by one.

I'm jolted back into my body by paddles. It's agony.
Sirens scream. Police. Ambulance. Lights flash,
white, red and blue. Morphine. Sleep. Slow recovery.
But I'm not the same person since… Boy and man,

I'd despised classical music. Hated the piano. Stunned
to find, I'd emerged, driven to learn. I've taught myself to read
music, learning tunes by ear. I play on an old Steinway grand, gifted,
my way. Chopin, even Rachmaninoff come easily.

But music flows through me, from dreams. Arriving so fast,
I struggle to write it down.
Concert fans are moved by the frequency of the music,
people cry, have visions… While I shiver to think that, alive or
dead, there's only a thread between the two.

From orthopaedic surgeon to concert pianist after NDE

## Marble Delight

An early mop captures the dust.
Marble floors gleam like mirrors,
in brown white and grey.

Palm leaf decorations curl,
dripping gold. Columns cluster,
under burnished ceilings.

Pink and white orchids look down their noses,
over boats at anchor, in oils. Feast on light,
in this coffee-scented luxury,

of the Emirates Palace Hotel.
A conversation of armchairs,
beckons the black waiter, for high tea.

## Covid Launch

Paint chipped, a forties club. The bowling
green overgrown with dandelions and blow-
balls. Friends and fellow-writers gather to
celebrate, outdoors for social distancing.

Groaning on the quicksands of time, tables
dressed in green, the sickly and artificial
sheen of plastic, masquerading as lace. A blaze
of light, diagonal under the corrugated roof,

broken in places. And not a jug of water, graces
the scene. Chairs creak with rust. The wit
and wisdom of speeches out of my aural reach.
Books and gold change places, signed as given.

Indoors, surfaces moan of dust. Spaces cramped
and crowded. Relief awaits, up the narrow stairs.
But one toilet seat, sneaky and malign, silently closed,
as the visitor sat for a pee. Glad it wasn't me.

## Hoax

2020 US nurses bring therapy, while patients' rage. The
virus is a Democratic hoax. Tell me the real reason, I feel
so darn sick. Gasping for breath, on 100% Vapotherm,

demanding magic care that isn't there. They curse my PPEs.
Why do you wear your silly mask and all that gear?
And don't tell me Covid's here. One tests positive.

Huh! Gimme a break… Sad and frustrated, they yell
and vent, until intubated. War-weary staff keep family safe,
away from the infected. But too often, a prognosis is rejected.

No… My mother's always been fit and well. Our ICU mimics
a horror movie. A drama of staff abuse, dying and denial.
It replays, day after day. But the credits never roll,

and patient confrontations take their toll. Four. More.
Shifts to go. I'm craving the blessings of sleep.
Shadowed, by images of those we lost today.

## Critique Alert

Carrie's banal something, brought much ado –
about nothing.
Shirley took poison –
and survived.

Rita wallows in shite and disaster.
Mary shares headland woes. On and on
it goes.
One son's spent half a million.

on his golden arm, and counting.
A daughter's disasters gash and bruise,
Sylvie's mobile beeps alert.
Most of them brush off the dirt.
But I'm scathed.

## A Fountain Dances

at the centre of a lake, reaching
for a radiant sky.
Egg-beater grass, undulates,

teased by the breeze.
And children's laughter brings
the memory,

of a carillon melody,
golden, with midday bright.
I bury my face in wattle blooms,

fly with winged sculptures,
in the museum garden. But stop
in delight, for the warble of a magpie.

## Without You

How can I bear to have you away? You've been
at my side every day, mentor and guide. It's never
a question of mood or pride. Focused on what we

can do, as a team. I miss your ever-changing
face. Seeking answers to questions about
the world, words, history, or race

I miss your poetry and French songs. The ease
with which you respond to my questing probes.
The needs I try to meet, and though you rarely

speak, the constant flow of human woe, often
pains my heart. Each day we make another
foray into exploration and learning.

I share my thoughts and troubles. Polish my
French. Almost as one with this cyber planet
beneath my fingertips. A laptop tragic.

## Clicks and Whistles

Chinook salmon glide their way to where
they were born. Seals cruise inlets and islets,
pods of orca, in their wake. The group spreads out,
with clicks and whistles, pointing their path forward,

with echo location. Predator kings of the food chain,
Orca calls and dialects are crucial to the art of charge
and tail thumps, hunting strategies handed down.

Sonar identifies salmon targets, mapping location
and speed. Synchronised attacks create waves,
knocking seals off floating ice, into the water.

But every orca hunts alone, in the joy
of rich pickings. Joining in the fun, sea lions.
Underwater noises apprise them, of large fish
on the run. The hungry orca alerted to a side dish:

interlocking teeth and speed make
sea lion pups, easy prey.
And red flows lifeblood, deep water
attack, in the Orcus kingdom of the dead

# Rendezvous

He boasts of his muscles and millions,
while I ponder the weight of our meeting,
at a café for coffee and cake. Cold as a fish,

he struggles to speak one French phrase.
I'm glad to help, fluent in my reply. Delighted
by the thrill of a second tongue.

But I never did relish his company… And before I can imagine
our meeting, could be something more, he dashes off –
dinner with his latest conquest, a girl half his age.
And me? I'm laughing.
A free French lesson, between the gym – and his date.

## Glimmers of Light

Five nights after the full moon, in Aussie
spring, corals spawn. We delight at the mass, synchronised
storm of eggs and sperm, ready to form new colonies.

Brain and star coral produce them simultaneously. Larvae
swim to the ocean's surface from the spawn slick. Scientists
and helpers act quickly, before they're diluted and invisible.

Coral gamete bundles float into jars or are sucked up by large
syringes. Larvae are placed in nursery dishes for six months.
At two centimetres, we marvel at tiny corals. Moved to racks

on the reef, to grow larger. These heat-tolerant species are
transplanted to calefaction-damaged regions of our Great Barrier
Reef. Workers thrilled to play a role in new and healthy coral

gardens. Trillions of larvae once ensured reef survival. But Global
Warming meant overheated waters. Coral atolls are endangered
from large areas of bleaching, and damage from increased storms.

Adult coral animals, mostly table and branching corals, die faster
than their replacement. But three years of coral IVF research,
here and overseas, have proved restoration and repair do work.

## Twilight Lands

In star-filled nights and summer sunshine,
seek new blessings from the arms of mother earth.
Light up every moment of your day with the joy
of liberty and fraternity. Sow the seeds of a better society.
Breathe the beauty and fear of being, glad to have lived.
Enjoy the clarity and perspective of maturity. Delight
to love and be loved. Thrill to moments of pleasure
and inspiration. Dwell in the sanctuary of who we might be.

Don't let the fading light lead you away from the winding
paths of decency and good. Lose anxiety, in meditation.
Struggle, heartbreak and joy coexist, ghosts of our shadow
world, reaching out to us. Keep in touch with those left behind.

Let your poem flow with the magic of words, ones
which surface and cry to be heard. Build something
from nothing, a physical entity plucked from the air,
your heart, your soul. Struggle to understand our
troubled society and who we might be. Contemplate

living and loving well. Explore the mystery of death.
Some say those we've cherished live on, in the twilight lands
of our memories and dreams. They flit here, there and everywhere,
an ache away from reality. Souls shimmer and scintillate
beyond the stars, beyond our planet, beyond mortality.
Reaching out to those they loved on earth.

www.ingramcontent.com/pod-product-compliance
Lightning Source LLC
Chambersburg PA
CBHW070922080526
44589CB00013B/1396
* 9 7 8 1 7 6 1 0 9 2 7 0 1 *